Published in Berlin, Germany, in 2023
by Fireflies Press
www.firefliespress.com

Design by ilhas studio
Typeset in Figue by Good Type Foundry and
Untitled by Klim Type Foundry
Printed and bound by Know-How

Images: p.8 *Ghost Strata* (2019); p.20 *Two Years at Sea* (2011); p.30 *Ah, Liberty!* (2008); p.42 *The Coming Race* (2006); p.52 *The Sky Trembles and the Earth Is Afraid and the Two Eyes Are Not Brothers* (2015); p.64 *House* (2005); p.76 *Sack Barrow* (2011); p.86 *What Means Something* (2015); p.96 *A World Rattled of Habit* (2008); p.108 *Ijen / London* (2022); p.126 *The Minotaur* (2022); p.136 *Krabi, 2562* (2019); p.148 *Slow Action* (2010); p.158 *Now, at Last!* (2018).
Courtesy of Ben Rivers, Kate MacGarry Gallery.

Distributed by Books at Manic (Australia)
and Idea Books (rest of the world)

ISBN: 978-0-6454547-1-0

The German National Library has listed this publication in the German National Bibliography; detailed bibliographical data is available at http://dnb.dnb.de



This publication is generously supported by Jeu de Paume and STUK: House for Dance, Image and Sound.

# Collected Stories

Ben Rivers

Fireflies Press

7
19
29
41
51
63
75
85
95
107
125
135
147
157
169

Daisy Hildyard
Kevin Barry
Chloe Aridjis
Vanessa Onwuemezi
Xiaolu Guo
Irene Solà
M John Harrison
Nathalie Léger
Helen Oyeyemi
Golan Haji
Marina Warner
Gina Apostol
Iain Sinclair
Lynne Tillman
Ben Rivers

# The figure on the wall

Daisy Hildyard

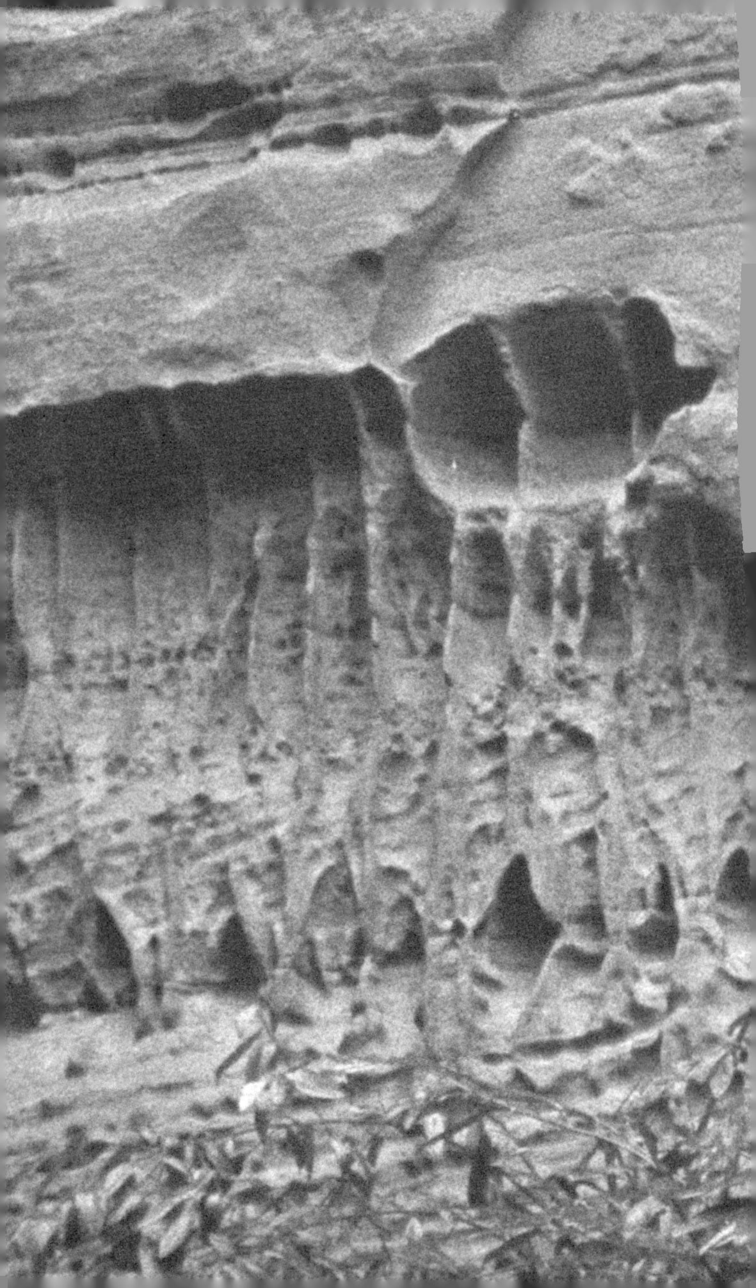

I am here to talk to you today about the work of Ben Rivers. Ben Rivers is a British filmmaker, the English name 'Ben' comes from a Hebrew word meaning 'son of' and the geographical term 'Ben', as in Ben Nevis, comes from a Gaelic word for mountain peak, or cone, which derives in turn from a word meaning 'projection'. I think you know what rivers are. Ben Rivers makes projections which can be shown on walls and screens in galleries and cinemas, or watched on a television, laptop, or phone.

Ben Rivers grew up in Somerset in the south-west of England and later lived in a small flat in Bethnal Green, East London, in which there was a sofa, a bed, a potted plant, some heavy cooking pans, and several pictures on the wall. We can say with a degree of certainty that Ben Rivers left light footprints in the dust around Biosphere 2 at Oracle, Arizona, when he was filming there. We can infer that miniature reflections of Ben Rivers and his camera have existed, fleetingly, in the eye of the sloth, the squirrel, and the birds he has filmed, even though these reflections were not necessarily visible to the naked eye.

There is some evidence of Ben Rivers in Tuvalu. When Ben Rivers was in Tuvalu he recorded footage of the heaps of rubbish that are piled here and there around the place, because there is nowhere otherwise to send garbage on this archipelago of small islands that lies low in a rising ocean. Ben Rivers's camera took a long look at these rubbish heaps and it also noticed several ingenious objects that the island's inhabitants have fashioned from repurposed trash. The camera's attention to these things comes to feel affectionate. We can assume that a very small proportion of the material in at least one of the rubbish heaps on Tuvalu is that of the filmmaker Ben Rivers himself.

In Ben Rivers's past, there was a time when sediments of stone settled down on the ground and solidified. People came, and painted on cave walls. There were novels and wars, people went mad and were imprisoned and argued for the rights of women and planned revolutions.

In Ben Rivers's future, people live on islands, biospheres, and below ground. There are swings made out of hubcaps. There are weapons made out of old sieves. The elderly put sacks on their heads and charge into battle through the hazel and cherry trees in rural Somerset. Every species is going for broke as usual. There is a stinkswamp and a dog swimming in the sea.

The person who watches these Ben Rivers pasts or sees these Ben Rivers futures may find her own versions of the past or future altered. In the present, too, she may find herself standing in the kitchen, looking strangely at her flatmate who is holding the kitchen sieve. These perceptions are all component parts of Ben Rivers's oeuvre.

There is a story by Henry James called 'The Figure in the Carpet', in which a journalist becomes obsessed with the overarching meaning that is hidden in plain sight in a novelist's oeuvre. The novelist himself insists that all his works are unified by a single subject or message, as a Persian rug features a repeated pattern. This figure in the carpet becomes the emblem of this profoundly meaningful secret of an artist's work, or perhaps it is a chimera, or perhaps it is a joke.

There is a short story by Virginia Woolf, 'The Mark on the Wall', in which the narrator becomes preoccupied with a mark on a wall. What is this mark – a hole, a stain from a dried rose leaf, a nail head – and what event, story, encounter or purpose does it attest?

At the beginning of one of his films, Ben Rivers draws tarot cards to predict his own future. He is offscreen, though we hear his voice and perhaps we see his hands touching the cards, or are they the fortune teller's hands? It is not possible to tell. We hear Ben Rivers ask the fortune teller for advice on his next movie, and she says, 'It's very funny because I would say it's about you.'

Another Ben Rivers film opens with images of prehistoric paintings on cave walls, including footage of the Bird Man at Lascaux in the Dordogne. The Bird Man, a figure with the head of a bird, the body of a man with a big erection, is one of very few human forms in any prehistoric work. Early artists depicted the gods and animals that surrounded them, rather than depicting themselves. Ben Rivers presents these cave paintings in black-and-white footage. The original paints, in brown, red, and yellow tones, were made from iron oxides, calcites, and manganese oxides, which were quarried by the painters or their people from the local area.

Manganese oxides are industrially quarried and processed today, and used in the production of stainless steel and batteries, which are necessary for the manufacture of cameras, phones, and torches. Ben Rivers can been seen on film guiding a torch in a darkened space over *A Rake's Progress*, a series of eight paintings created by William Hogarth in the 1730s. *A Rake's Progress* tells the story of a man's moral downfall as a series of still moments, marks laid down in paint by Hogarth but shown on film by Ben Rivers as a moving light show.

The Ben Rivers film that opens with the Lascaux paintings closes with a VR tour through a flat that Ben Rivers used to live in (a narrow bed, a view of the estate, a novel on the sofa). At the end, we see the simulated wall of this displaced habitat. It is strangely patterned with cracks, like an old painting or a building that is falling apart. On film, on this wall, a figure begins to draw itself. It becomes apparent, as it emerges, that this figure on this virtual wall, no more than a play of light, is that of the Lascaux Bird Man.

Ben Rivers's thoughts are made into work, and the work leaves a trail in the wider world. There are moving images of a moon diorama, horses in the sea, a naked bum, a person reading a novel in a quiet room, the breeze in the leaves making shadows on the curtains. There is fighting, there are drums, crowds of birds dipping over the water, bubbling tar-like substances, gunshots, whales singing in space, bare legs beneath a fig tree, old footage of actors and actresses suppressing their feelings. These are all constituent parts of Ben Rivers.

Ben Rivers's films have instigated many dreams. One evening, not long ago, a young woman watched a Ben Rivers film on her phone after work. When the film had finished it was past midnight. The woman made her phone go dark and placed it beside her, then curled up on the sofa to go to sleep, in her work clothes and bare feet. Dozing, she dreamed that she was a sloth having a trip. Her fur had rainbows and algae trapped within it. She was covered in multicoloured petroleum. The inside of a phone was her habitat and somebody had hit slow playback.

Ben Rivers has instigated beliefs, opinions, feelings, and an argument between a young couple. This couple had watched a Ben Rivers film in which a squirrel is seen interacting curiously with a model of a squirrel that appears to be made out of some rough wood or coconut shell. The couple, who had met online, were on their second date. After they left the auditorium they walked along the river, arguing about the squirrel: whether it was fighting or playing, and this led into another, more significant disagreement about art and the quality of reality. This couple did not go on a third date. This is yet another work of the filmmaker Ben Rivers.

Perhaps this couple will meet again and find a way to agree. Perhaps they will go on other, better dates. Perhaps they will be happier alone. The possibilities are endless.

The possibilities are endless. We know for sure that Ben Rivers originated in Somerset. We have floated through a flat he no longer inhabits, witnessing the pictures on the wall and the heavy pans in which he has made meals. We have gained access to the moon diorama, the political tracts, and the swimming horses inside his head. We can be confident that he has authored a situation in which a person walked across a projection as they took their seat, revealing, as they did, a large and very precise self-portrait in silhouette on the screen. We have heard Ben Rivers's voice behind the camera and seen many things and stories that his eyes have looked at and his mind has thought up. We have given our attention to the heaps of garbage to which he has contributed a small offering. We have seen the tarot card that he pulled, looked at, and returned to the pack. We watch but do not feel his hands impart warmth from his body to the card, and then we watch but do not feel the card lose this heat.

# A Season in Youth

Kevin Barry

In the last months of the century, when I had just turned thirty and was feeling as old as time itself, I decided that I wanted to leave the city behind for a while and head out west.

Over the course of the late summer I made a slow and staggered progress – the towns that I stayed in kept getting smaller, and the sky opened out to the Atlantic horizon, but still I wanted to go further on down the road.

I made out along a peninsula in the far southwest and then, as if at once, all the people disappeared, and then the trees went, and I was left to just the stone grey hills, and the higher mountains in the distance, and the sea.

The sea ran on thin ribbons of steel,
hard clean lines in the autumn light.

But still it wouldn't do for me – I wanted to go further out again.

Towards an edge, or a fall, or a precipice of some kind.

Maybe to an island, out there, just beyond.

Instead I found a sheltered place on the coast and I secreted a small caravan there. The days were short and the nights were mostly clear and full of the same old stars and never-ending. I tried to fill up the time with notebooks full of schemes and plots and ingenious nonsense. I tried to slow down the tense hours, and then slow them again.

There were draughts coming through the caravan windows – these were bone-evil in the night, and they skinned me alive. So I cut up a sheepskin rug and arranged strips of it to block out the draughts. I was precise and rational about the job, with a measuring tape, a steel ruler, a Stanley knife. I had the radio on and whistled as I worked. It occurred to me that I was patching up a nest in there, and I thought that it looked quite well for a finish, especially at night, with the candles lit, and the glamorous furred edges, and blue moonlight falling on the Caha Mountains, and what they were selling that year was loneliness.

Sleep started to come more easily and the days turned into weeks and suddenly there was the feeling of All Souls.

I dreamt recurringly of two black dogs creeping

low across the fields at night and woke always from this ominous vision in a slick of sweat.

But the morning came through and I could breathe again and the late grasses were taken by the silver fires of the early frost and I dwelled for a while among those bright October days.

The year's last temperate spell of weather drifted in from the ocean.

At noon of day the light was slant and stark and I could see all of the unbreakable things, and I remember some of them, too – I remember the spider as it clung to the bars of its wind-swayed web.

Sometimes at night when I woke I scratched down some words in a notebook by the side of my fold-down bed – nonsense words, half-rhymes, notes towards a character, and injunctions to self.

Once I woke and read these words and had no memory of writing them in the night –

*be a warm and generous man*

Suggesting that I was neither.

But I was changing even if I didn't know it. By the hour and the day I was shedding the last skin of youth, and taking on another.

And now the mountains were hard-founded in the sharp winter light. And now the sea groaned on its slow rusty cables. And now a new path was opening, and beckoning me onto it.

# Codex

Chloe Aridjis

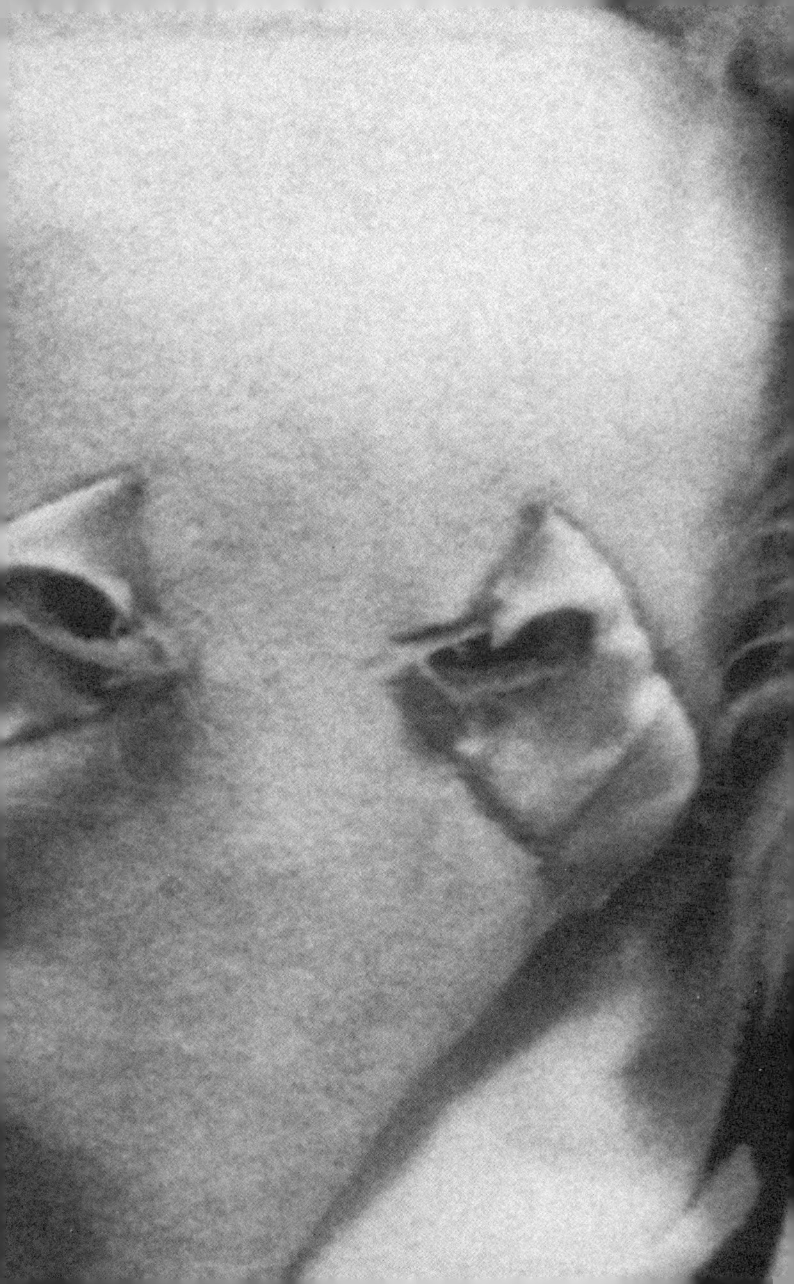

Of the few remaining documents of this mysterious civilisation over which children presided there is a rare manuscript, a folded accordion of intricately drawn scenes, illustrating the daily life and rituals of this vanished community that thrived at the foot of the mountains. If you carefully fold out the pages of bark, illuminated on either side, you can learn about this lost world and admire the transcription, written and pictorial, of the strange community our scribe happened to stumble upon during his travels through dense forest and voluptuous mountain ranges in a remote part of Europe.

The inhabitants of this civilisation appear to have been between six and twelve years of age. Despite their youth they carried out their daily lives with a purpose and determination characterised by the absence of rules. Our scribe paid particular attention to rituals, flora and fauna, mythology, and local beliefs. He was permitted to live with them (separately, in a camper van) for a limited amount of time.

Due to unknown and inclement circumstances the accordioned pages have since come apart at the seams. The subjects have become scrambled. What follows are a few of the scribe's observations, albeit not in the organised presentation of the original.

~

It began with a stroke of lightning, a divine intervention from above: the adults, ensconced in their metal carapaces, went up in flames. Yet every now and then one of them still appears. He wrecks the equilibrium with noise and slaughter. These raucous grownups must be dealt with accordingly.

The children do not worship any god.

The children regard the mountains as their elders; they alone can remind them of the true measurements of time.

The land undulates from one horizon to the other, free of the structures that try to possess it and pin it down.

The children receive their knowledge from the silences that thrive between mountains, stones and trees. The youngest child is especially adept at other languages and put his ears to the ground.

Additional thoughts are sometimes

> gleaned from the conversations of laundry strung up across the yard.
>
> Other coordinates are more open to interpretation, such as the overflowing bathtub: a baptism carried over from the lake or a magic spell gone wrong.
>
> Mountain crests, rooster crests.
>
> An imaginary goddess, mother to all children and animals, is said to dwell in the mountain slope's lowermost cave.

Among the examples of flora that thrive in the region the following were noted:

> Almond trees. Apple trees. Aspen. Bramble. Bulrush. Cedar. Chestnut. Clover. Cockle flowers. Columbine. Dandelion. Elm. Jasmine. Laurel. Lemon trees. Myrtle. Narcissus. Olive trees. Pear trees. Thistles. And three willow.

As for the children's animal companions, our scribe had some difficulty establishing the exact relationship between the different species but noted down the following:

At night the dogs circle the campfire. They carry the secrets, the donkeys promise interpretation, and the roosters expound at the crack of dawn.

During the day, the dogs take the pulse of the land. They alone are aware of both the dangers and the possibilities of every crossroads.

The dog of the east predicts a great conflagration.
The dog of the west predicts most nights will be tranquil.
The dog of the north predicts strange arrivals.
The dog of the south has no interest in predicting.

Reddish horses graze on a hill like brooding cave paintings.

An iguana pauses at one of many thresholds. The creature inhabits its own astronomy, aware of darkening clouds and of a dust that has started to absorb the light from distant stars.

And within their own astronomy the children trace their own constellations (forever retraceable) and wear a multitude of faces.

Each face channels a different ancestor.

The children are particularly responsive to the ancestral.

The children are like little volcanoes that never erupt.

They dance, masked, in the junkyard's fevered dream.

They explore the eccentric debris of a past civilisation, a cemetery of journeys that came to an end.

Here no one is king and every ruin is a throne.

*See what we have done, see what we have done.*

Captivity is a mired vehicle. And a mask you can never remove.

> But freedom is spelled out in the glowing calligraphy of the campfire, and in the outstretched arms that encompass an entire horizon.

~

Our scribe remained with this mysterious community until one day, alerted by a thunderstorm that the end of the world was nigh, they asked him to leave. It is unclear whether the children stayed on in their kingdom forever or whether they migrated to other climes once they entered adolescence.

# 2006

# Vanessa Onwuemezi

Stargazing and a string of faces: ashen, worried, wondering, shying, colluding. A string of faces and still no sound mouthing the hour, no sound of the hour striking.

Still no hope of yesterday returning and yet, and again yet. Around I will walk through the vermilioned dryness around again, and yet to cross the horizon again. Our feet turn the Earth and we move, again the crack of rock splitting, the broken path, the smoke from the fire, the pilgrimage up towards     this year, next year, again.

The quietness of the rock has bottomed me out, made me deep and hungry as a well so the depth reaching along those bottomless openings in the ground spew up, dust and steam, redness spread around as cloud, the air blue forgotten, and we breathe in, we walk past.

Still no sign of the hour turning.

All this loneliness and no one to share it with. We are each the crown of the pine tree, or the palm, each and one to ourselves. We are each that twist of rock molten and reformed. Each come to our own mountain and slip a lonely path under force of the starling's stink and buoyant song, under fear of the dark wet caves and the downpour  the shriek of bats woken from their sleep O we envy their fearless sleep. This is only the beginning of the race.

The calm before the running. When we will heave a body of noise over the ridge disturbing the gentle airways through which the mountain breathes, and has us  holds our weight. For all the stargazing we cannot see them, the precious animals that should point our way at night – the pig, the dog or water rat – just a string of faces in the sky, worried, rushed, forgetting, colluding, determined, shying on their last ebb of faith and so on. And so on and on, with a grimace and mouth open, dressing ourselves in shadow, hooded eyes, concealed and blurred expressions and so on and on.

This is what it is.

And take a breath of dust and say this is  this is my slice of happiness, and say, there was never anything so lovely as this and say – we dare not say more.

We dare not say another word. We take each other's hands and  we are naked. And feel each other only through the skin and sweat which amplifies the sense of ease flooding us at the sight of the sea. Finally we have our bearings and finally, we can and for once stop, a moment, and pick at the clusters of pink tubers, the crunch of the seabed underfoot, and eat up the sounds of this life crashing into the next. Never mind the one who sits alone because that's him.

That's him, isn't it? In the eye of his own creation. With gaze sloping towards the ground then drinking up the sea that's him, we know. With the moon for a little while. Who both looks and sees through the one eye, and we eye him. Glancing off our skin is the hardest light. A tree on a white beach. He is. A coconut shell in the rock and on, so on.

And finally we climb and we run. So he has coloured everything in a melancholy tone, in a trembling, shimmering, artificial light which draws lines around our pores and gives shape to our senses, to the hairs on our arms and growing from our heads. Light that reveals the sometimes harshness of our year, but then still its slow hazes and pulsing seas who lose their thoughts to our minds. Who whisper through the grey rains drunk up in restless gratitude.

We hope that the mountain will hold us.

That it will not shed us in a landslide, a sigh and roll of rock, and keep us waiting under the stones marking the time on our fingernails and peering through the gaps up at the red sky, the wounded moon, unable to take the beauty of it. Unable to take the memories O the heavenly dips and flows of stone. The little bird wings. The sharp of their beaks dipping to the water to drink. Can't take the menace of the sun's shadows our whole journey is in shadow, still no sign of them turning the hour and yet, and ever yet, the first light is our returning faith, which overnight was buried, but never lost.

# The Feminine Desert

Xiaolu Guo

The name Sahara is derived from the Arabic word for desert, in the feminine form. I think of a woman prostrate on the earth, her tears mixing with the sand, and the wind barely ruffling her hair. The woman in my mind's eye is doubled. One is Sanmao, a Chinese writer. The other is Isabelle Eberhardt, a European writer. Both were in love with the desert. Both died by the desert's hand. Both are my heroines.

Sanmao, born during the Sino-Japanese war in Taiwan – it was not because of the war that Sanmao left for another continent. It was because of her mind. Her wild mind. I am not sure if she met Paul Bowles, though both lived in the same desert. Perhaps once they passed by the same dunes, under the sheltering sky. In the desert the sky offers a refuge.

Sanmao was beautiful. But beautiful is an adjective that offers nothing specific. A tacky word cannot describe such a woman. Her beauty was the virtue that created her writing. She was larger than life. And her writing was larger than life. But contained by life. Life in Chinese – sheng huo, 生活 – is more evocative. Sheng huo means to be born and to strive.

Sanmao lived multiple lives in multiple languages. In Chinese, in German, in Spanish, in Arabic, in a Saharan dialect. Multiple lives demand we slow down the memory machine.

It was 1993. I was in Beijing to study filmmaking. I was twenty. I experienced the desert wind and sandstorms for the first time in my life. The capital was under assault by yellow winds from the Mongolian desert. The wind from the west. The Jundu Mountains in the North China Plain did not shield us from the desert wind. Nor did the Great Wall of China. The desert kills, buries, and forgets. The desert dries, removes, and shimmers.

Then I read Sanmao: *Stories of the Sahara*. The author confessed that from an early age she avoided writing the character Mao – 懋 – in her name. Containing twenty strokes, it was too difficult to write. So she changed her name to another Mao, simply: 毛 . She called herself Echo. Everyone needs a new name.

There she was on the cover of her book. In a white Moroccan robe standing against a vast desert, her long black hair tangled in the wind. High cheek-boned and barefoot. And her husband José, a Spanish marine engineer, with a bushy dark beard. The perfect pair, a proud gypsy couple. Young, hippyish, almost primitive. They blended with the dunes and camels. They had encounters with the people of the Sahara, and the colonialists. They scavenged for food and witnessed tribal life, encountered child brides and brutality. All in simple prose, infused with a tragic sensibility that only a woman brimming with wanderlust could transmit.

All Chinese literature reads like travelogues. When one travels alone, one writes, without the accelerations of planes and cars. What would you do in those long dark hours, on horse carts, or in train carriages? Reflect and record.

A woman far from home and her own language. And time passes. Time measured by the wrinkles on one's face. And time passes differently in the desert. It might not pass at all. I travelled with her, Sanmao, the wandering soul, throughout my university years, knowing that she had already killed herself some years prior, in China. She wrote those stories in her prime, when José was healthy, when the desert was still bearable, still liveable.

Years later, I came to Britain, and read *The Nomad*. Isabelle Eberhardt died in the Sahara in 1904. She was a Westerner who dressed as a man and lived amongst the local Muslims. Eberhardt's diary, shattering, painful, and addictive. She was a francophone Swiss. Wildly attracted to desert life from her childhood, by the age of twenty she had converted to Islam and travelled to Africa, changing her name to Si Mahmoud Saadi. Yes, all of us need a new name. She wrote in a raw way.

I cannot find another word to describe her style. Raw, as in raw apple cider, full of zeal and fervour and choked with life. She cried out: 'I will never be content with a sedentary life, I will always be haunted by thoughts of a sun-drenched elsewhere.' Elsewhere, always elsewhere.

Accused of being a spy for the French, Eberhardt was hated by the Algerians. She was stabbed by a Muslim soldier and narrowly escaped death. Perhaps she was regarded as an enemy, a colonial symbol, or, simply, a woman who refused to live in a womanly way. She was damned. Yes, a white woman from Europe, what was she doing there, in the desert on the back of a camel, dressed up as a man and carrying a weapon? No good. That wild girl.

She wrote and travelled in a man's robes. Only three years after the stabbing, she was killed in a flash flood in Algeria. She was crushed under her mud house. She was twenty-seven years old when she died. The diary of Eberhardt is the only writing I have read by her.

When I read Sanmao, I felt as though I was under gentle rain on the shingle beach. I was soothed by the evening wind on the dune. When I read Eberhardt, I felt as if a knife was stabbing me in the stomach. An exaggeration. But not quite. Pain cannot be quantified. Very different effects. But both are powerful. I mean, the gentle rain and the stabbing pain. Sometimes the gentle rain can cause pain, heartbreaks and deadening sorrow.

You might ask, what is the connection between the two women? Is it the desert? Is it because they were women who lived extreme lives? No, it is something else. It is about belonging but not possessing. It is about surrendering to something bigger than the self, larger than the human world, surrendering to it but not claiming or conquering it.

The sky trembles and the earth is afraid, and the two eyes are not brothers, wrote Paul Bowles.

Men talk. Women nod their heads. Men answer. Women listen. The desert is silent. The woman is hushed. The desert is unpredictable and volatile. The woman's mood changes like a sandstorm. The desert kills, buries, ruins, and forgets. The woman cries, laughs, yearns, and throws her body onto the sand.

The sky trembles and the earth is afraid, and the two eyes are not brothers.

I am back in my university dormitory. I lie with my head on the pillow, in a bunk bed. The dormitory is shared with four other girls. The loudspeaker is blasting communist songs. I am reading, but not Sanmao, not Eberhardt. I am reading about the desert. Yes, the desert itself.

My mind is rushing through the multiverse. The desert does not remember any of our lives. The desert does not speak our languages. The desert speaks all languages but not ours. The desert is not an anthropomorphic being. I refuse to translate every object or every natural being into a human language. It is not in English, or in French, or in Spanish, or in Arabic, or in Chinese. The desert is the desert. You can find yourself in the desert. But the desert is never yours. The desert is never mine.

# I've Been Thinking About Houses Lately

Irene Solà

What happens to a house when it is left alone? It becomes worn and aged. And its paint peels and its foundations begin to sink. It goes for too long unlived in. What does it think of? What does it dream? How does it regard those creatures who built it? Who brought it into existence only to abandon it when its usefulness no longer satisfies them. It may grow lonesome. It may stare for long hours into the darkness of its empty halls and see shadows. Its heart may jump as it thinks, 'Here, here is someone again, I am not alone.' Each time it is wrong. And the hurt starts over. It may haunt itself, inventing ghosts to walk its floors, making friends with its shadow puppets, laughing and whispering to itself at the end of some quiet cul-de-sac. It may grow angry. Its basement may fill with churning acid like an empty stomach. And its gorge may rise as it asks itself, through clenched teeth, 'What did I do wrong?' It may grow bitter. It may grow hungry. So hungry and so bitter that its scruples dissolve and its doors unlock themselves. While a house may hunger, it cannot starve. And so in fever and anger and loneliness, it may simply lie in wait. Doors open. Shades drawn. Hallways empty. Hungry.

– *Anatomy* (2016), Kitty Horrorshow

I've been thinking about houses lately. I've been thinking about the act of choosing a parcel of the world. Choosing it well. Making sure that the sun looks down on it for most of the day. That it doesn't flood when it rains. That a slight cool breeze passes by it at dusk. That it's not a corner where the earth groans and burps, nor the den of some other animal, or the little door through which dozens of earwigs and hundreds of ants go in and out of their pantry. That it's not encircled by an insomniac highway. That it isn't the meeting point where a group of motorcyclists test their exhaust pipes. Or where local teenagers gather in the wee hours to drink and listen to reggaeton.

Then, put up walls and a ceiling on that little patch of open land, a foundation, a chimney, windows. Shake the hand of the man or woman at the real estate agency. Pay three months of rent; one is the entrance fee, another the deposit, and then the first month. Say 'mine'. And close it up like a walnut. Like two tense hands imprisoning a bird. Turn a key, secure shutters, draw curtains, and breathe peacefully, because we are safe, there inside. Warm and dry. Sheltered. Protected. Take in another breath and release it. As if the mysteries, the darknesses, the beasts, the fears, the strange sounds, the evil and the desperate sounds, the cracks, the crunches, the creaks, the murmurs, the terrible things that hide in the dark stains between the lamp posts, as if they respected those sorts of rules, or didn't know how to open doors or slip under them, how to climb stairs or push elevator buttons.

Then, lock up our things, inside with us. Books and other objects. Boxes and bags and suitcases. The food we eat and the smells of the food we eat. Tools. Clothing. Dreams. Nakedness. Sex. Some stories. Some conversations. Sometimes, letting one of those things get out, momentarily escape, stick out a thin leg and show it to the morning, to the evening, to the night. Eat or drink or piss or laugh or cry or take off our clothes and sunbathe or make love in the garden, in the forest, in the street. Take outside mugs and forks, a tablecloth, the computer, eyebrow tweezers, notebooks, pitchers, towels. Label some of them rubbish, never to come back inside. But keep the others, the ones that are ours, tucked into a little box that is a house.

The personal things. The ones that belong to us. Or that we decide belong to us. And they condense, there inside. Day after day, week after week, like a thick soup. Heavy. More and more meals have been eaten on the same table. More books read in an armchair. More dreams dreamed on a pillow. More crying, more laughter, more sneezes and coughs, more vomits, more conversations fill the rooms. More and more crumpled shop receipts. Scraps of paper. Hairs in brushes. Stains on mirrors. Until one day we leave, or we die, and we take our things with us, or they are taken out. But we don't take them all with us. We can't possibly take them all. The ones that can't be seen, the ones that elude our grasp, the ones that remain clinging to the walls, the ceilings, the nooks, between the tiles, in corners, they do not leave. And the house is left empty, some would say. But there are no empty houses. There are momentarily tranquil houses. Seemingly tranquil.

When I say I've been thinking about houses lately, I mean over the last few years. I've been thinking about houses and I've been living in houses, and I've been living in houses while thinking about houses, and I've been accumulating and storing things inside houses, and not only the houses that welcomed my body – my eating body, my sleeping body, my heated or calmed body – but imagined houses. Any house, but particularly an imagined house, is made up of many houses. Make-believe and actual houses function in similar ways. Doll houses. Toy houses. They are all similar. They contain stories and they contain life and they contain events and anecdotes and trivialities and details and ideas and bodies and words and objects and memories, which we could also call ghosts, which we could also call thick soups.

Most houses are very patient. Because only rarely is a house in a rush. Invulnerable to rushing, and to tickles, even when invaded by dust, or spiders, or five kids with five flashlights, or new residents. Invulnerable to shame, even when its shabby innards are revealed, even when its bulging ceilings are pointed out, its crumbling staircases, its peeling walls. Even when they say, 'How filthy, the people who lived here before,' 'How idiotic, whoever put that switch there,' 'How incompetent, making the sink like that,' 'How careless, to stain or scratch or tarnish this floor, this wall, this marble,' 'How tacky, choosing that wallpaper, that bathtub.'

And I've also been thinking about ghosts, lately. I've been thinking about intruders. About new inhabitants of a house and about old inhabitants of a house. About a house that is big enough, and flexible enough to hold all sorts of tenants, small and big, permanent and just passing through, hirsute, hairless, fugitives and dawdlers, of flesh and blood and without flesh or blood, pleased and angry, naughty and curious, legitimate and defiant.

Because I will tell you one thing: it's very comfortable inside *this* house. Perhaps it's the silence. Perhaps it's because it is a fickle, fathomless house. Like all houses.

Translated from the Catalan by Mara Faye Lethem

# notes for an imaginary

M John Harrison

> I always arrived after the workers, and would leave before they left, so I had an impression that they never left, continuously going through these precise motions.
> – Ben Rivers

1: The Unidentifiable Crystal
Twelve minutes or so into the film we see, without warning or preamble, half a woman in a royal blue overall, in another room, framed by a doorway or perhaps doorways. There are tubes. An ancient mirror that doesn't reflect anything but dull light; and in the background a wire, draped at exactly the same angle as the visible part of her shoulder. Everything else is squared off. There are sounds: something like a vacuum cleaner in a more distant room than the one we're seeing, and then sporadic drips and clicks, recorded in such close-up that they distort and echo.

2: Four Wires Enter a Milky Fluid
From the first image, in which we come upon drums of chemicals, stacked beneath the handmade sign 'Sack Barrow', to the last, in which a figure – seen through the mismatched panes of a grimy window – limps slowly away from us, this film is full of quiet yet faintly menacing non-events. It feels like a history, though it is com-

posed and presented as a record. And if the film feels like a history, it isn't just the history of the building but of itself. In the record we make of the film we might note: 'Ancient, rusty, furred-up pieces of machinery, operated by – and this is shocking in some way – ordinary human beings'; then, 'some kind of corrosive steam filling the air'; and 'unidentifiable crystals scattered on all surfaces'. A man wears an old-fashioned overall, an old-fashioned heavy work glove; a woman winds wire. There are sudden inexplicable bursts of music. A bell rings but you're not sure why. Fumes rise from acids, perhaps as they have always done. How we'll interpret this record later isn't obvious. If it feels like a history, it also feels like the preamble to a fiction, a setting that's already testing its own realities.

3: Nostalgias & Responsibilities
Those drums, those baths, those fumes. You would be very cautious about moving around in here until you knew what was being made, and how, and what for. You might be told; as a viewer you might be fully informed. But you suspect you would never really know. Instead, excited yet at the same time calmed by repeated partial scenes – repeated partial activities – you begin to guess. What is your responsibility here? The

little old factory is closed now. Even its name seems old, the name of something you might find on the side of a moorland hill: Sack Barrow. It is like a building in a fairy tale. As a viewer, what contribution are you expected to make?

4: A Mysterious Visit Beneath the Waters

Light falls on things but you don't know where it originates. A woman reads a passage from Herbert Read's novel *The Green Child*, in which a couple descend into the watery labyrinth that extends beneath the world. 'Time and its anguish were abolished.' This is spoken over images of acid baths, and of a man in a hat who seems to be listening to her but then is seen to be speaking to, laughing at something else. He's not even in the same room at the same time but part of the extensive, inexplicable something else that contexts all these events. Is that a bell that rings? Speech and music are distanced, muted by a distance you're not quite sure is actual. How can things this close be so far away? How can things so certain be so impressionistic? How can things so certain be so tentative?

5: The Sack Barrow Imaginary

A man seems to be ironing. He isn't, but he might be. He might be ironing his clothes in a one-room flat. All the men who work here, you think, live in one-room flats. You consider this assumption for a moment or two, then, without having come to a conclusion, move on. The men have pinned up photographs of attractive, energetic, agitatedly smiling young women; they play old music – Workers' Playtime music – and potter about making tea. Everyone here, man or woman, has managed to domesticate this environment enough to be able to visit it day after day, like the couple in the mysterious underwater bubble in Read's novel. 'Smoke Gets in Your Eyes' comes over the radio from the past; then 'Pretty Flamingo'. At this point the men's eyes especially become sentimental and remote. At this point, you wonder if both the anarchist novel – with its spectacular visit to the watery labyrinth beneath the earth – and the mysterious Sack Barrow of the imagination, can only be seen as keys to something else. Some other perception.

6: You Would Be Very Cautious About Moving Around in Here

Ben Rivers retrieves an unfathomable quietness from it all, despite the noise. The little workshop closed in 2011. All of these processes, we have to assume, were automated long before that. In factories elsewhere, every object or method we see here has certainly been left behind, allowing us to forget, for convenience, that modernity can't leave its precursors behind since it develops entirely from their efforts – those efforts which, in its effort to centre itself, modernity now interprets as wrong, insufficient, estranged, out of date. The other thing modernity can't leave behind is that all projects like Sack Barrow depend, at root, on the respect for work Rivers locates so carefully and depicts so well.

7: The Past Re-Runs Itself Again

That scene, with the partial woman in the royal blue overall: I watched it on Vimeo. I could run it again and again in the attempt to develop my understanding of what it offered. Why do I prefer to remember it as this quick, barely retrievable glimpse, this combination of chaos and absolute precision? What did I see? What was it for? Everything in that little factory used to be there. It was there – it was present – for many years, from 1919 to 2011, providing work first to the returning veterans of World War I, then to people who simply found it difficult to fit in anywhere else. Now it's gone.

# The Frame of Mind

Nathalie Léger

## 1.

The story of young B. encountering Peter Handke on a station concourse and, stunned by this apparition, unsure of how to introduce himself, exclaiming: 'It's me, I am your Reader!' The story of H. asking Gilles Deleuze whether he could attend his lectures, and eventually confessing: 'But I've never read your work.' and Gilles Deleuze, relieved, replying: 'At last...!' Jacques Derrida meeting the young student Avital Ronell and, intrigued, asking her: 'But who are you?' and she: 'I am Metaphysics.'

These are only examples. If there is an *aleph* on this earth, a point in space which, as Borges tells us, contains all the points, it isn't in the basement of some ancestral home, but rather in the geometric centre of this inconceivable, hypermobile figure one mundanely calls – mundane because that's the point – an encounter: the mass of illusions and coincidences, the mass of intentions and representations that projects itself into a focal point invisible to the naked eye.

Other well-known examples: Motherwell on the threshold of Rothko's studio (thinking he won't be able to come in), Rauschenberg knocking on de Kooning's door (hoping he wasn't there), Emin entering Bourgeois's place ('and she was in there'), or yet Clouzot recording Picasso, Koralnik in Bacon's lair, Namuth filming Pollock, but also Beckett scrutinising van Velde, or Genet, Giacometti. The gap, the interval between the ones and the others. What then becomes perceptible of the darkness, the speed, the boredom, shoes, fixity, dust.

2.

He doesn't really know why he has asked her this, and she doesn't know at all why she has accepted. The framework is set. Enter Rose Wylie.

To say that he has placed the camera here rather than there doesn't suffice. He has placed it. Two systems face each other. At the beginning, being bold, one would be tempted to say, like Foucault beholding Velázquez's portrait of himself painting the portrait of the king: 'To all appearances, the place is simple; it is pure reciprocity.' To all appearances, Ben Rivers beholds Rose Wylie painting a picture which at the end beholds us. They are both perfectly familiar with the long history of all this, but neither of them is interested in mise en abyme or demonstrations, let alone in lessons.

It is completely serious. They're tackling this together. They don't have the same subject, but they have the same objective. To capture, try to capture – what? Time, hypotheses, stalling, stubbornness, 'and embarrassment', Rose says; to flick through the images, to examine them from all sides, to catch the faces of women, the faces of tyrants, to wait. I'm trying to capture Ben Rivers who's trying to capture Rose Wylie who's trying to capture – what? We can't say, we can't name it. She repeats. What we seek, we can't name it.

– *Next?* she asks.

3.

In his *Natural History*, Pliny the Elder recounts that the artist Zeuxis 'painted a Penelope in which he seemed to have represented his own frame of mind' – which is what Ben Rivers does when he films Rose Wylie. He shows his frame(s) of mind. No need to enumerate them, one example, very short, will do: clap – this convention, the action that marks the beginning of a take. Clap. What Rose does with it. Her unconcerned, mildly bored manner despite her wish to do well, the dance-like gesture with which she agrees to begin. Rose consents to enter the film, but not to enter her own portrait. She is present, but she is remiss; she plays the game, but she is elsewhere. But where? Precisely where one is at work, that is to say, the place where no one is looking at you. Rose Wylie. When she enters the frame, it's with the idea of getting out immediately – that's one of her frames of mind. Not the least. Ben shows this.

'What force is there in the thing one gives that compels the recipient to return it?' asks anthropologist Marcel Mauss in his essay *The Gift*. 'Deep down,' he says, 'these are mixes. One mixes souls into things; one mixes things into souls. One mixes lives. That's the contract, that is the exchange.'

She doesn't really know why she has accepted, and he still doesn't know why he asked her.

*What means something.*

Translated from the French by Cécile Menon

# Introduction to a Stone

Helen Oyeyemi

Saturday July 1st, 2023

Dear Ben Rivers,

I hope this letter finds you. I can't think of a reason why that wouldn't happen, but on the other hand, there's no real reason why it would.

An acquaintance of mine recently tried her hand at improving the quality of the culture I consume.[1] This acquaintance forwarded me links to four of your films and wrote that if the faceted light that sparkles from these compositions doesn't reach me, she'll consider me a lost soul. So there was some suspense. A search for a soul, even. Mine, yours, anyone's. Well, it was the quickest game of hide-and-seek ever. I pressed play on *A World Rattled of Habit* and pictures breathed in and out before my eyes and ears, each

---

[1] We were discussing our most anticipated films of the year. I was like, '*Barbie*, duh.' Looking as if she couldn't believe her ears, she said: '*Barbie*? But what about *Oppenheimer*?' I explained that I can't keep up with the cascade of imaginative works devoted to death and destruction, I told her I haven't even got started on any of those Netflix serial killer biopics yet… I don't think my acquaintance bought this excuse, but she had to leave it there. We could insult each other for hours, but it'd be a waste of time. At the end of the day there are multiple methodologies for looking into the depths of being, no? And more than one way to be bored, or entertained, or whatever. Hence: the summer of Barbenheimer.

silence paired with a sound, each pairing perfectly natural in the imprecision of its intervals. As I watched, I heard somebody clear their throat.

It wasn't me, but I didn't look around. I was thinking that if I'd imagined that 'Ahem', the situation would develop according to its own desire, and if I hadn't imagined the 'Ahem' then I could deal with it later. Onscreen, shadows, drumbeats, birdsong and footfalls drifted over faces and objects like gold dust (but a grainy and gravelly gold). I was listening to Oleg mocking time and place, I was absorbing leaves and quizzical questions, and – 'Nice to see you, sorry I got old,' Oleg said. Then somebody who definitely wasn't me went beyond throat clearing and said, 'Huh.'

This happens to me sometimes: I used to take pills so that it wouldn't happen. The medicated years weren't bad, but they weren't great either. When I reflected on the kinds of things the pills stopped me from hearing, it became clear to me that my main reason for wanting the medicine was the way that people would react when I told them about the things I heard. It was mostly the external reactions that had depressed me, not anything internal. So I stopped taking the pills, resumed listening, and kept my findings to myself and a select audience. You've got to have a feeling for the right people to tell, that's all.

Anyway: when I heard the cryptic 'Huh' whilst watching *A World Rattled of Habit*, I had a few theories as to who was speaking, and I said 'So now you feel like talking, eh?'

I was operating on the assumption that the only objects in the room would be the ones I'd spoken aloud to lately. I'd recently critiqued the capacities of a teacup and a vase and had subconsciously been expecting them to say something back, something like, 'Yeah, well, look at *you*.' But the 'Huh' hadn't come from the flawed teacup or the unsatisfactory vase, it had come from an object that was quite far down on my list: a heart-shaped stone I'd questioned at length and had all but given up on getting any sort of response from. I could feel that the stone considered me too stupid to understand anything it said. My questions, all of which were variations on a theme, probably proved the stone right.

I couldn't help it, though. You see, this stone was acquired in the desert in eastern Georgia last year. I was walking along with two people, and one of them saw this stone in the sand, picked it up and handed it to me. I was – and am – greatly affected by the shape of this stone, because in the months before this desert trek I had been in a lot of mundane pain for a lot of mundane reasons, I'd had a summer of lying awake with the fiery sensation of my ribcage clenching and cracking open, and the toll this took was of course more than physical. It didn't seem possible that I could have any heart left – based on those night-time experiences all that remained was burned jelly. But then autumn uncovered a stone shaped like a heart; I rubbed sand off it and didn't wince.

The voice that had said 'Huh' asked if there was 'any more where that came from'.

I said, 'Any more where what came from?'

'I meant... are we going to watch any more of them films?'

'Oh. Yes.'

We watched *Phantoms of a Libertine* and *Krabi, 2562*. And the sense of a watchful 'we' was palpable, what with the occasional chuckle and requests to rewind, pause and perch our attention on certain instances of temperature fluctuation, warmth and formality between temporary companions, the shy appearance of the macabre in the conversations of children.

Eventually I asked, 'Who am I speaking with, by the way?'

'Oh... I'm the stone you brought home from Kakheti last year.'

'The heart-shaped stone?'

The stone muttered something.

'What was that?'

'Nothing. Forget it. I knew it was a bad idea to talk to you.'

'No, what? Just say what you want to say. Have you got some sort of problem with being heart-shaped?'

The stone said it wasn't even heart-shaped. It said I was the one who decided it looked like a heart – a kind of third-hand decision, in a way, since its shape doesn't bear a resemblance to any anatomical heart, but is closer to a crayon heart drawn by a five-year-old in a hurry.

The stone told me its shape doesn't mean what I think it means, and added that it didn't want to talk to me because it didn't trust me.

'Nothing personal. I just don't get on with people who insist on putting things into words. They get it wrong and then deny that there was any other way to say it... It's annoying... and I'm busy...'

'Busy with what?'

The stone said it preferred to keep its daily activities private.

'Then what do you want? Why are you speaking up now?'

The heart-shaped stone[2] asked to be introduced to you.

---

[2] I take the liberty of still describing it in this way since that's how the stone inhabits my mind, and besides, the stone probably isn't going to read this letter.

‘With a view to what? You feel like you’re ready to leave Prague, is that it? Auditioning for a role in Ben Rivers’s future work? I didn’t realise stones could be ambitious in that way.’

But we talked some more, and I think I get it now. The stone simply wants you to know that it exists in this world. On the desk beside my laptop there is this stone that recognises something in your art and its way of delineating the currents between people and things, occasionally halting at the question of what exactly one thing has to do with another, sometimes flowing past such constructed complications. If your films act as go-betweens, so too does this stone.

Okay, now that I’ve written the letter I promised I would, I’m off.

Yours sincerely,
Semiramis Sacheverell

# The Smoke

Golan Haji

# I

The way a foundling bumps up against his mother in the veins of a tree, a blue moment bumps into you inside the veins of time.

How many dawns couldn't prepare us for the day to come, how many yesterdays in which we were surprised by a roll of thunder, although the shepherd had predicted that for tomorrow, raising his licked finger to the eastern wind, saying: 'it will not rain today.'

The sweet word which we received confirmed in its beauty the certainty of our departure. Through the years brief messages with jumbled dates addressed us, but not by name, mocking our early arrival or reproaching us because we were late, by fifteen minutes or a thousand years. Not once did we realise where these messages came from, or who the anonymous sender might be; sometimes we showed them to passing strangers, apologising for the obscurities, and when they stopped to look at the screens held in our hands they'd see nothing

## II

With sharp smiles we stabbed the proud night, its mighty silence, so it ripped the gut strings between our roots and our wings that we'd thought were so strong.

The song fell away, but not the wind

No land is calmer than this one that is filled with our absence. Neither books, nor trees. Nor complaints.

Love that outlasts the night.

He who has all this soil on his tongue will stay silent

## III

Our language now is defunct, we invented it by inveighing the animals, and loathsome as the stench of history's boarded-up cupboards, it became foreign even to us, like an error or a threat – chirruping its coughs, weeping its questions, laughter the mother of knowledge...

I can explain myself to a sparrow, you are terrified that grass might understand you

Our dialect is buzzing in the air, the faces of the listeners tight-shrink to a fist, perhaps because the drought has almost shrivelled our tongues, or when we see we simply can't speak

We were the witness to the extermination of
words and the survival of rules

Like the wire of a broken lamp

Speckled by the faeces of flies

Every speck a remnant dot of 'i'

IV

The world was a mirror woken by the moon so that the images flooded   we shouted 'your here' & 'my here' like two bullets ricocheted by people hidden in the dark   we sat down to ponder our roles   we contemplated the images and they contemplated us   we waited for them after farewells and they waited for us on the walls we burned them and the smoke brought tears to our eyes   we gazed for so long that fatigues overwhelmed us so the pebble became a stone and the rock another stone   we could no longer put a name to what we were seeing   we proliferated despite ourselves, we multiplied our faces so as to amuse others & to entertain each other mouths and eyes opened about us like the brass spigots on wine barrels   poisonous waters of the deep flowed toward our thirst–

Those dark distant waters' unheard bubbling under all that we see, they rise in autumn like the growl of a prayer in the tower of a temple

A shining name adhered to you as light does to
foam

Between the sun and the nightmare I was the
eyelid that revealed your naked pain and closed
it off again

We didn't sleep alone, our old refrain came back
to warm us

Breezes opened and shut the veil of the sky

Like iron that craves rust & rain we were evaporated by the force of nature and we soared into the future  we snaked through its narrow opening that was guarded by scorpions  our tomorrow was here before us  we roamed through its wildernesses, scraps of extinct novels that raged with tragedy and troubles  we couldn't forget how prudence had rotted our desires, how we sighed stained by the silence of others

V

We stuttered when we said, smiling:

'How pretty is the life of our enemy

Their inferno brimming with roses'

We will not die as long as water flows

We are the grandchildren of the river–

Our patience is unending

Our hopes higher than confined time

In a wheel-barrow with a broken wheel

We carried the wounded world

To the sty

We toiled like mules

We were disdained for long years

We were what surrounded us

We ate sulphur salted with our sweat

Our excrement shone like stars & suns

Even the fears of your insomnia came true:

The full moon spat in my dish

Except for this mother solitude

Where could we have gone to

With all of our solitudes

When we begged the goddess of our far-away river

Kneeling before her so she could take our hands in hers

The waters of our memory defaced us

VI

On the remains of a road shimmering with cold glances of water you shouted:

'I swear on the Seventh Heaven I will strangle my big fear with my bare hands – I will grab this great serpent by its head and break its horns and put out the cinder in its mouth with my spit!'

No one saw the battalion of angels with their huge wings lift up the great fear that you'd slayed dragging it with silver chains to Mount Qaf  its tail ploughing the earth in September its fangs digging through the Seven Hills a road that reaches the horizon  the dust of our ancestors, they who were proud of us, a cloud trailing behind it:

You were born of ‘No’ – your beautiful tender
mother

Loosed & delighted, as if in a steam locomotive with its windows open to the apple orchards going from the onset of spring to summer’s end

A new life hasn’t started yet crowned by ants, deaf as this rock, seen but not sayable

Cursing the one who led us with his wisdom to this height: ‘The first step these ruins, the last, annihilation.’ We were afraid until the glances of larks shone in our eyes, their brightnesses revealing us in the earth that camouflaged us. We returned to where we had run from carrying Thirty Shadows heavier than our names, boasting that we alone had prepared ourselves for this return–

Like a stork standing wide awake on one leg on its nest on the chimney of a hospital, ruminating on what it might scavenge from the marshland in the harsh times

You were ripened by the long hours of silence
under the sun

We disappeared to turn back  we cut roads through time like outlaws  we illuminated them with the velocity of our collapsing  those as ignorant as we were relied first on the compass used by swallows with heads lowered because the venerated stars are under our feet  but the road is cunning  it knew us but we did not know it  it crossed us but we couldn't cross it  the road waving at us from far away moving us from its right hand to its left   we are held still between its arms.

I raise my eyes from the feather that landed between us suddenly as a sword

The mountain had to disappear in order to stay, its kingdom everywhere

## VII

The sun above us

Red as wine is

Rotating with the keys in its hands

Naked with our grime under its last light–

I on the summit of despair

The empty word my lost house

You in the lowest depths of your hope

Behind your eyes a mirror

Who appears in it is shattered

Scattered between us

The bones of secrets we buried

Even dogs

Disdain what we once thought of as great

VIII

The vertigo of galaxies & the vertigo of existence
made my loneliness dance

Neither brothers nor mourners

My youth a sickle that harvested my soul

There the earth is a swing on the waters

That lulled my father to sleep

So my mother might be born of
his most tender rib

You who are on the throne

And in the river threw the cradle of His beloved

You granted me this bundle as a chair

To rest my elbows on my knees

Banished far from the fate of my brother

Outspreading my hands as if I were an
outcaste

As if I had assassinated all people

I am exiled to the Moon

To carry across the country of assassins

The bundle of thorns until all
people are resurrected

The smoke escaping the fists of witnesses

Rising up to You

My body the sacrifice

A burning spike of wheat

Let the clemency of Your gaze ensheath me

Disperse

me

in

the

silence

of

Your

silence

Author's note: it may help to know that the final section of the poem (VIII) includes references to two suras of the Quran ('The Table' and 'The Smoke'), *The History of al-Tabari* and the second canto of Dante's *Paradiso* (from *The Divine Comedy*), where the Lord banished Cain to the Moon, condemning him to carry a bundle of thorns until the end of time.

Translated from the Arabic by Golan Haji and Stephen Watts

# Blindsight

Marina Warner

The queen woke up laughing one morning and the king asked her what was so funny. She pretended to be fast asleep and didn't answer straightaway because she wanted to hold on to the delicious feelings a dream had given her. Her sleep could often take strange flights: one night a bushy red beard had sprouted all over her face, and on another she'd soared up in the air with scythes for arms. She'd found them rather heavy to beat and she'd planed down, waking abruptly on landing. But on this morning, she sank back into the new dream's voluptuous embrace, it was so delightfully ridiculous and wicked.

'I just had the silliest dream,' she told the king.

He flung a heavy arm around her and patted her bump contentedly. 'It's going to be a boy, I'm sure.'

She knew better than to say more.

The strange contraption her dream self had stepped into was 'bespoke', said the man standing by, giving her a louche smirk. He looked like their odd-job man, so very adroit he could fix anything, and was leering frightfully as he harnessed her into his device and hoisted her up. 'That way, lady, you can reach him without any difficulty.' *Him* was... she laughed again as waves of intense pleasure lapped at her once more. But her merriment was soon mixed with growing unease and she dug herself deeper into the bed and began to think back to the scene and the startling depth charge it had delivered into the core of her body. The mind has such weird twists and turns, she marvelled, and then shivered. A bull! Who would ever have imagined she could be enamoured of such a beast?

As the dream pictures fragmented and vanished, shame broke through the glow of initial delight and guilt began to creep over her, and with guilt, fear.

'Look, bless you, what a prince!' The nurse held up the squalling baby and placed his hot little body to her breast. He was still naked and slick and slippery from his exit into the world, and she had seen with a jump of joy that he was indeed a boy, with everything in place as well as thick dark curly hair, masses of it, swept into swirls by the amniotic grease and other juices. His eyes were closed, with long lashes curving down his cheeks, and his dear snub muzzle was scrunched up from the squeeze down the birth canal.

At that moment, the queen felt a rush of passion more intense than the joy that his two sisters had excited in her before. 'My treasure. My wonder, you funny little thing,' she whispered, kissing his brow, where two buds were starting to form.

The princesses came in shyly to meet their newborn brother. 'He's awfully furry!' said one, putting her hand gingerly to his curly head. The other sister shivered as the shock passed through her and she cooed, 'Oooh, you are a little beast!'

A ferocious protectiveness rose in their mother. 'All newborns are like that, she said. It's called lanugo... It'll fall out, you'll see.'

The prince was a voracious suckling, who pummelled his mother's breasts with his fists to bring down more milk. The queen loved him for his neediness, and cossetted him possessively until the prince could stand, when the princesses vied with her to fuss over him. Little mothers, they dandled him, petted him, walked him, tied ribbons in his pelt and on his still budding horns, they bossed and chivvied him. He was their plaything, their slave, willing to do anything they told him, always running after them to be in on their games; when they hid from him they crowed at his bawling. They'd shove and poke him during a round of blind man's bluff, and race with their gaggle of friends to take all the seats in musical chairs and leave him out. His older sister, whose long limbs and tendrils of sun-bleached hair excited his passionate adoration, and who would, in due course, betray him to the man who would kill him, now kissed him and then laughed – 'Loser!' – and dashed off to join the others.

'You're too young to be with us,' they'd say, 'and you're such a lout.'

Although he bit back his tears when he became the butt of their high spirits, his grief was yet more bitter when they ignored him.

The king looked on coldly and muttered about being surrounded by women, each one more foolish and wayward than the next.

All went forward without serious harm, during those early years. However, as he grew chunkier, heavier, ruddier and hairier, he'd underestimate the impact of his bulk as he launched himself on one or other of his tormentors. There were incidents. Injuries. Complaints made.

It was her fault, the queen knew, her ungovernable dreaming, and she was frightened – for herself, and for her child. Her husband, looking daggers at her when the report of another incident reached him, hinted he had plans for the boy's future.

And that handyman, so ingenious, always watching her. Was he ogling her? No, she checked herself, anxiety was driving her crazy.

She was expecting the worst when the king

woke her one morning and said, 'About that moon calf of yours.'

She remembered with a shudder how Oedipus was spiked through the ankles and left on a stony mountain.

Once again as she slept, the handyman appeared, obsequious, knowing. He was wearing his leather apron, clanking with tools. 'Lady,' he spoke in a sad undertone. 'I know a way to keep him out of danger.' He paused. 'I have in mind a special kind of playground. A puzzle, a riddle, a life-size board game!' He held up a model, a toy of wax and twigs and grasses. 'He'll be able to play there, and no harm done. He'll find a way out, if he's clever...' He let the sentence hang.

It was a solution. 'Anything that will keep him under control,' her husband had said.

# Passing Beauty

Gina Apostol

I watch Ben Rivers and Anocha Suwichakornpong's *Krabi, 2562* with the detachment of my familiarity. I grew up in a Filipino beach town. I know those Thai sandscapes, its tourist-bait folklore, local ennui, Hollywood lures, and soda-pop commercialism. But as I watch, each cut – ingenuities of sound footage, narrative subterfuges, visual dislocations – rivets me. For one thing, every shot is beautiful. The mundanity of a father and child sipping drinks on a motorcycle, monumental crags of mythological caves, even the comic appearance of a modern Thai Tarzan sloshing amid waves to sell soft drinks in a commercial shoot is framed with seemingly offhand symmetry so that the juxtaposition of a pink, bland umbrella with the haunted glamour of a misted sea is ordinary, jarring, and right. This jarring beauty suffuses *Krabi, 2562*, a movie about dissonance and disappearance. There is always a sense of transience, of beauty that passes before I notice, and when it is gone I wish that I had captured it. Then I realise, the movie already did. So here is an attempt at describing this passing of beauty that the movie offers.

At its base, its beauty comes, of course, from the nature that it captures not only with its camera's lingering eye but also, very moving for me, its extended sound cuts: I hear a rooster before I see it, and the river's insects even after the camera has left sight of water. As someone who grew up with those sounds, the way IRL for me as a child nature seemed to reverb in Sensurround, the movie's crafty sound design tells me: these are filmmakers who not only see but listen. Listening is an art this movie foregrounds. What plot it unfolds lies in interviews with no questions, just responses. We listen for clues about a woman's disappearance from a receptionist, retired boxer, tour guide, movie theatre caretaker, anonymous workers of a resort town milieu who are the movie's Ariadnes, spooling threads that may or may not get us, or the woman, in or out of the tourist cave, the labyrinth.

An aspect of that labyrinth, the film's plot, is moviemaking. The film's patient pace, its correct insistence on allowing a shot to prolong, meditates on the act of filming itself. The film's beauty also comes from what is not nature, from what is technological and constructed – the movie's cross and parallel cuts seam its trifurcated scenarios: a woman's tourist trek through a resort town, her goals unknown; the making of a commercial; and the gestures of survival of what appears to be an aboriginal or prehistoric couple, who are the movie's nub. The presence of the couple provides not only a veritable, plausible historical haunting but also a historical cause for filmic cuts. For instance, an image from one scenario, depicting the commercial's shoot in front of ancient, mythological crags, is joined to another of the disappeared woman trekking through what could be either simultaneous or parallel – and beautiful – folkloric crags. In this cut, the film uses geology as splice, which both confuses and calms, making us wonder: is it the same place but different time, or the same time but different place? The movie makes sense and un-sense out of the seamed scenes, so that part of its detective plot, directing the viewer's enquiry and gaze, is the mystery of the stitching of film itself.

But it's the presence of the silent, aboriginal couple, bound to their cave and to the rhythms of nature, not in a saccharinely soulful, moody, or grieving way, but in an offhand, casual, even cursory way, so that the camera seems only *slightly* curious about their habits, that ties the movie together. We see them first through the commercial Tarzan's flustered gaze. The actor taking a leak and the Indigenous man meet in the tropic trope of a paradisiacal forest. Through the piss haze of the drunken actor's eyes, what's primeval at first looks like a haunting: a ghost, a supernatural monster amid his world's natural bounty. But the camera's lens on the Indigenous couple is matter-of-fact, documentary, and inverts our conception. The couple are ordinary. They fish in the same waters that for the commercial are only a backdrop and they are perhaps the last local witnesses, un-interviewed, of the woman's waterlogged trail. In the figure of the couple, the film's beauty also comes from its political undertow: the twinning of land with history, and nature with its *contra-vida*: capital.

Submerged, underwater, is the story of what settlers have done to the land, in which the ordinary modern citizen, or receptionist or tour guide or market researcher or film director, is part of the plot of settler colonisation. The simultaneous presence of the Indigenous couple – a man silently roasting his caught fish and a woman patiently watching – with the movie world of the comic Tarzan and the tourist world of the disappeared woman of mysterious aims (they could be artistic or unethical, familial or commercial, charming and/or invidious, all at the same time) produces the movie's logic. That is, the logic of its cuts, its beautifully unexplained transitions, its ambiguous nature sequences, its unerring, unsentimental, and generous eye on local colour. On the one hand, this simultaneity of a couple who seem prehistoric, even geological, with the very modern presence of an independent city girl and her twin, her fellow outsider in Krabi, the dazed movie-actor Tarzan man, is the film's commentary. Our personal epics and mysteries, what drives us to go trekking beyond our homes, are not separate from historical and still ongoing Indigenous removal. More obviously, blatantly, and yes, always, absurdly, outrageously, the selling of commodities is a direct cause of historical and ongoing Indigenous removal. The movie corrects the modern fantasy that we are haunted by history: history is a presence, among us, roasting the fish it has caught over a real fire.

But this simultaneity is not only polemic, a commentary. When I finally emerged from the movie, I realised what riveted me was the way that in *Krabi, 2562* meaning and means are the same. Simultaneity is both *Krabi, 2562*'s argument and its art. As I mentioned, in the shots there's a sense of transience, of beauty that passes before I notice, and when it is gone I wish I had captured it. And then I realise – the movie already did. What *Krabi, 2562* does is stitch through filmic measures how our world, both man-made and natural, is revealed and unseen and in danger, disappearing, before our eyes. But its disappearance is no mystery. For after all, Krabi, its ordinary people and supernatural caves and breathtaking beaches, is still here with us, and we know our human depredations even as we visit, partake, and tour. With Ben Rivers and Anocha Suwichakornpong's camera, we see beauty passing: their camera is witness, but it is a wise one; it knows that the beauty of what is nature lies not only in our environment but also in how at each moment we must look, with the dawning recognition of what we have done. Glimpsed too late, we wish to capture it as it goes – the fragmented, seamed, stitched memory of our presence, whose consequence still passes us by, eludes us.

# Never Too Late

Ian Sinclair

*'Never too late.' The slow approaching and amiable assassin, messenger of mortality, speaks to the old lost man in the park. The bare feet of this benched veteran are dew-sodden, dirt streams between prehensile toes. He is staring with such naked hunger, century-tired oyster eyes, into the shivering skirts of an established tree. The bitter thirst of the green desert is almost appeased. He is quite drunk, staggering on a sugared tease of wisdom. And overwhelmed by the excitement of running his fingers through subtle grooves of bark. Now a casual exchange interrupts the purity of the art of morning. This is an original and repeated moment of surrender, rooted and stalled in honest London earth. Outstretched arms become branches. Nails are budded. The pilgrim is isolate and mute. He is absorbed into the glorious nimbus of that which can no longer be seen, must not be seen, its outline lost.*

*'Never too late.'*

*Foolish laughter. The challenger flaunts a wiry scurf of beard beneath the visor of his tight mask: the photograph of a photograph of a nameless illustration in a French encyclopaedia, victim or criminal. The ironic commentary is deployed as a lulling gambit, before the killer strikes. A comment on the vanity of continued existence. A well-intended and final warning. For one and for all, place and man. On a condemned planet losing momentum. Losing interest.*

*'Never too late.' Never too late until it is.*

My father amputated the limbs of miners trapped deep underground, clawing and scratching at coal measures derived from ancient forests. His own father had come here from another and colder country. They took no payment from those who had nothing to pay.

Armed with a 'British Bull Dog' revolver, the Webley .450, my medical grandfather piloted his motorbike through massed strikers to reach the surgery where he would treat their wives. Nothing in the action of that creeping past is easy. Narrative has no respect for posthumous sentiment and revision. What happened continues to happen, slower and slower on each cycle, until it stops: this dream called life.

Mines fail. Memories are flakes of yellow newspaper in the wind. Ancestors no longer walk in our sleep. Although no printed record can be found of this mysterious interlude in a voyaging biography, with many months, out from Tilbury, spent at sea, my great-grandfather was changed, perhaps enlightened, by those fabled days drifting through a chain of unmapped Pacific islands and coral atolls. His own crimes, if crimes they were, evolved from poverty, expulsion, too much reading, and too intensive a love for the crops he planted, the yield of the land, the miracle of exotic growths in impenetrable jungles. The crisis of the rapids, holding him back from the whirlpool of dead forefathers, marked the end of a chapter. The story, cast adrift on a fast-flowing river, is left for others to complete. Our grandfathers are voiced in stone, in waterfalls and articulate smoke.

Having visited the former coffee plantations and all the verifiable Latin American locations, verifiable by map and photograph, my father, retired from his medical duties, plotted his voyage into the past, the last he would make. 'Life on the Society Islands,' he read, 'is predominantly novelistic.' By sailing in quest of Edens promoted by Stevenson and Conrad, but undescribed by his own grandfather, he wanted to access that privileged zone between the written and the unwritten, between transcendence and karma. The dreamlike drift of abdicated duty, the nights of brilliant stars, would permit him, so he hoped, to become the self that he might once have been, ancestor of his ancestors.

Warriors, he understood, were allocated forty-two years. That was the number of the house he had inherited from his father. The house where his son was born and where he grew up, trying to absorb the view from his bedroom window, a rim of rounded bluegrey hills, replenished slag-heaps, conifer plantations.

'Never too late.' Except that it is. Heart flutters. Driving licence suspended. Voyage postponed. Indefinitely. No more stairs. The world is a garden. Untended. He gathers provisions by taxi. He slumps, weary, shopping bags around him, in the red Naugahyde chair, the gift from grateful patients on his retirement. The room is now the island, the books and the fetishes, the grave goods brought back from Peru by his grandfather. It's done. But the stories those places tell, the astonishing feats of navigation by the people of the islands, cohere and continue.

*With the abacus of stars, those nights with no possibility of landfall and no desire for it, the reverie of death is revealed as a sequence of flashing numbers. Forty-two, the allocation of years, doubled: a life and a half-life, a ghost life folding back to an oceanic beginning; of constellations beneath the surface, depths where the only illumination is the decay of undiscovered plants. Plants that need no discovery. Plants without names. Count them. Forty-two is the number on the door. Forty-two is the number on the door where the William Burroughs impersonator arrives with his flask of bug powder in the film of a book assembled by other hands. Eleven is significant too. It is the day of his only son's birth.*

*Forty-five minutes is the span of time for which he takes responsibility. The messenger is waiting. 'Never too late.' He starts to write. After forty-five minutes on a kitchen clock, he will stop. The rest goes into the stream. The rest is left with 'silver-tongued strangers'. With noble pirates. With the dogman haunting the park. And murderous priests fishing with dynamite.*

*After the Great Storm, uprooted trees floated downriver, each one containing the germ of a forbidden book. In the mists of autumn the ship casts off from Tilbury. The pub is called The World's End. Our story begins. Corpse fishers net the wrong man. The drowned come ashore asking for forgiveness. 'The petrified skin of an impossibly ancient body.' Ruins are heaped on ruins. 'Never too late.'*

# MAYBE

Lynne Tillman

He stood in a corner of the large room, hoping not to be seen and also wanting to be, his usual ambivalence, the party racing, the booze going fast, a cool desperation, he thought. If he tried, he could imagine her at the party dancing sinuously, throwing her head back, her movements flighty and also deliberate. She knew what she was doing, and standing here, stuck in a corner, he could visualise her the way she was back then, when she was with him, and of course she wasn't anymore, and might never be; she could be anywhere and with anyone, or content to be on her own, stunningly independent. It seemed interminable, though, the time he was kept waiting, hanging on until she declared... What, though, her undying love. So he cut... the umbilical cord, his analyst said, which, back then, twenty years ago, felt inappropriate. This isn't funny, he said to the analyst, who went silent, but now it was funny, though he usually regretted any retrospective-mindedness, it didn't help. Prosaically, he had travelled in one direction, she another, insufficient reasons that would do, he told himself, because the heart has four chambers, each with its own rhythm, and feelings are way more complicated, and sometimes so mixed they can suspend your life, even paralyse you.

She bothered him in a silly way, she didn't interest him any longer, or he didn't feel he could hang on to what she offered him, a paltry dish. Her new life, what she said she hoped for, discomforted him and didn't align with who he thought she was, so maybe she wasn't what he thought, but do we know anyone else. Maybe she no longer wanted or needed his attention, and he didn't wait around to find out, didn't pursue her the way a fervid lover might have, instead he hung back. Anyway we lost our momentum, he thought, holding his empty tumbler of scotch, if love needs to keep time. He refused to be the one to make decisions, he wanted to know he was wanted. She was anxious about getting somewhere in life, where he wasn't sure, where is there to get to, really, he said to her. She called it a better place, to do something worthwhile in life, find her passion, all of that California stuff, he thought, and moved incrementally toward her and away, in too different a way. She wandered off, he felt, and even if she was present, she was somewhere else.

Surprisingly, in the gap of lost time, he entered medical school to become a heart surgeon, which she thought was amusing, but again he wasn't laughing, people in his family died young from heart disease, it was a good reason, but then she said he hadn't waited for her to make up her mind, he was too hesitant about her. He wondered if she would be a good life partner, he thought that way then, and time was his to take, wasn't it.

He was imagining her at the party: was someone there who incited these old memories, someone who looked like her or said something she might have. He stood in the same place, one hand over his heart, waiting for orders to change his position, but didn't know where he could go except to the crowded bar, drink more, forget to remember. You have got to decide, she said once, or maybe twice, sometimes you just have to take a chance, not look around to see if others agree with you.

Some people had left, most stayed, they didn't know what to do, either, where to go afterward, while the host began gathering dirty glasses, but the party was full enough, people talking, loosening up, nudging each other intimately, some kissing, swallowing tongues, so likely his lassitude or anti-social behaviour, as she had called it, wouldn't be noticed. Quiet, he blended into the darkening sky in the window behind him.

He might have asked, do you want to live with me, should we move in or on, will you marry me. Something had stultified him, the prospect of commitment, she said, but he might not understand her, maybe she didn't love him, or maybe she did in her way. Maybe even now he existed in her spell, in an abstract way, after she went her way, far away. His memories remained the same, resolute, they didn't change, frozen with the years, and there must be something wrong about this, he felt. Their time, the past, their past, pictures just images, blurrier with time, still unreeled almost relentlessly.

He pictured her as if the day before, the last time he accidentally saw her on the same line for a movie, which had formed into two lines, a popular movie, what was it? The lines were dragging and, when he saw her on the other line, dressed in black leather, her face rounder, her broad cheekbones fierce still, her dark blue eyes, he moved toward her to embrace her, but she repulsed him, she wouldn't give him a stupid, phoney hug, there was no them now, nothing, she had rebuked him. Some apologies come too late, when loving again is ridiculous, she could have said that, and yet it couldn't be. She was fixed in him, he must be in her, she must still love him, how could that have gone.

He looked around the room, emptier now, his third wife was talking to a man he didn't know, looking intent upon whatever he was saying. Maybe he should go over and introduce himself, break up their little conversation, assert himself, though he was content to watch, an onlooker who didn't possess her, his wife could do what she wanted, even complain about him, how he let people walk all over him, not bold enough, not enough for himself, and, worst of all, she said, he was slow to understand her needs.

She was, he noticed, enthusiastic, listening, laughing, captivated, then, awakening to a sudden recognition, he thought, she's going to divorce me, when did we last have sex, but maybe I'll leave her, I might, I could. Something was missing in his life. Maybe it was always her.

His friend Gene once told him, people surprise you, never forget that. He didn't expect surprise, life had a regularity, his hours regular except for emergencies, though his wife might surprise him, shake him up, and maybe that's what he needed, maybe they needed surprise, or escape, or to get a divorce. Maybe she was holding him back, maybe he could become – people are always becoming – happier, a different man. And when he was different, even if his transformation was slow, it would happen, and he, unencumbered, would contact her, and she would have had a change of heart, realised it was him, she loved him, then the time would be right.

Emerging from his reverie, he looked out at the room, emptier now, his wife smiling, talking to the same man. He studied her. But still, he thought, maybe he thought.

# Afterword

Ben Rivers

Reading fiction and poetry has been one of the greatest sources of inspiration for me since before I even had the thought I could make my own films.

I have spoken about this many times, but have never had the opportunity to bring it into direct relationship with my work. Following the invitation of Jeu de Paume, who gave me the opportunity to consider all my films in one season, the curator Antoine Thirion felt that this was a good moment to bring them into conversation with writers who have directly or indirectly informed them.

I drew up a wish list of living writers and, deploying some locational detective work, wrote to them, proposing they might like to watch a particular film (selected in the hope it would be of resonance) and to respond in any way they chose, with no necessity to describe or even refer to the film in question. This book is the result of those requests. Every contributor has responded with great generosity, brilliance and insight, illuminating my films in ways I could not imagine, while creating texts that exist in their own right.

I would like to thank all the writers concerned, the translators Mara Faye Lethem, Cécile Menon and Stephen Watts, and the invaluable connections provided by Gareth Evans, Cécile Menon (Les Fugitives), Viktor Palák and Jacques Testard (Fitzcarraldo Editions).

GINA APOSTOL has written five novels, among them *Insurrecto*, named by Publishers Weekly one of the Ten Best Books of 2018, and her most recent, *La Tercera*, out in May 2023. She has been awarded the Rome Prize, the PEN/Open Book Award and two Philippine National Book Awards. She grew up in Tacloban, Leyte, in the Philippines, and lives in New York and western Massachusetts.

CHLOE ARIDJIS is the author of three novels, *Book of Clouds*, which won the Prix du Premier Roman Étranger in France, *Asunder*, set in London's National Gallery, and *Sea Monsters*, which was awarded the 2020 PEN/Faulkner Award for Fiction. Chloe has written for various art journals and was guest curator of the Leonora Carrington exhibition at Tate Liverpool. Her most recent book is *Dialogue with a Somnambulist: Stories, Essays & a Portrait Gallery*.

KEVIN BARRY is the author of four novels, including the forthcoming *The Heart in Winter*, and three short story collections. He also works as a playwright and screenwriter. He lives in County Sligo, Ireland.

XIAOLU GUO FRSL is a Chinese British novelist, memoirist and filmmaker. She has published several novels and her memoir *Once Upon a Time in the East* won the National Book Critics Circle Award 2017. She also directed a dozen films including *How Is Your Fish Today?* and *UFO in Her Eyes*. Her feature *She, a Chinese* received the Golden Leopard at the 2009 Locarno Film Festival. *Radical: A Life of My Own* is her most recent nonfiction book.

GOLAN HAJI is a Syrian-Kurdish poet. He lives in France.

M JOHN HARRISON is a writer since 1965. His latest book is *Wish I Was Here*, a fragmented memoir. He lives in Shropshire.

DAISY HILDYARD is author of two novels – *Emergency* and *Hunters in the Snow* – and one work of nonfiction, *The Second Body*. She lives in North Yorkshire.

NATHALIE LÉGER is an editor, curator and writer. She wrote *Les Vies silencieuses de Samuel Beckett*, followed by the trilogy *Exposition*, *Suite for Barbara Loden* and *The White Dress*, and *Suivant l'azur*. She is the director of the book series 'Le Lieu de l'archive' and 'Diaporama', published by IMEC. For Les éditions du Seuil, she has edited Roland Barthes's courses *La Préparation du roman* and his *Le Journal de deuil*, among others.

VANESSA ONWUEMEZI is a writer living in London. She is the winner of The White Review Short Story Prize, 2019 and her work has appeared in literary and art magazines, including *Granta*, *Frieze* and *Prototype*. Her debut short story collection, *Dark Neighbourhood*, was published in 2021 and was named one of *The Guardian*'s Best Books of 2021.

HELEN OYEYEMI's books include *What Is Not Yours Is Not Yours*, *Gingerbread*, and the forthcoming *Parasol Against the Axe*. She's a recipient of the Somerset Maugham Award and PEN's Open Book Award, and her novel *Peaces* was shortlisted for the Goldsmiths Prize. She lives in Prague.

IAIN SINCLAIR has lived in Hackney, East London, since 1968, working on a delirious theory of everything, by way of poetry, film, event curation, novels and speculative essays. He has published widely through mainstream and independent presses. His books include *Lights Out for the Territory*, *London Orbital* and *The Gold Machine*. In film, he has collaborated with Chris Petit, Andrew Kötting, Grant Gee, John Rogers.

IRENE SOLÀ is a writer and visual artist. She has written the novels *Els dics*, *When I Sing, Mountains Dance* and *Te di ojos y miraste las tinieblas*, and the poetry collection *Beast*.

LYNNE TILLMAN's latest work is *Mothercare*, an autobiographical book-length essay. Peninsula Press recently reissued her novel *Motion Sickness*. Her essays and stories are published in *Frieze*, *Aperture*, *Tank*, *n+1*; and she writes about contemporary artists for museum catalogues and artists' monographs. Tillman has received a Guggenheim Fellowship, a Creative Capital/Andy Warhol Foundation Arts Writers Grant, and the Katherine Anne Porter Prize from the American Academy of Arts and Letters. She lives in New York with bass player David Hofstra.

MARINA WARNER writes fiction, essays and cultural histories inspired by myth and fairy tales. Recent books include *Inventory of a Life Mislaid: An Unreliable Memoir*, and *Temporale*, a reflection on time in lockdown. She teaches Creative Writing at Birkbeck College, London.